This book
belongs to

....

....

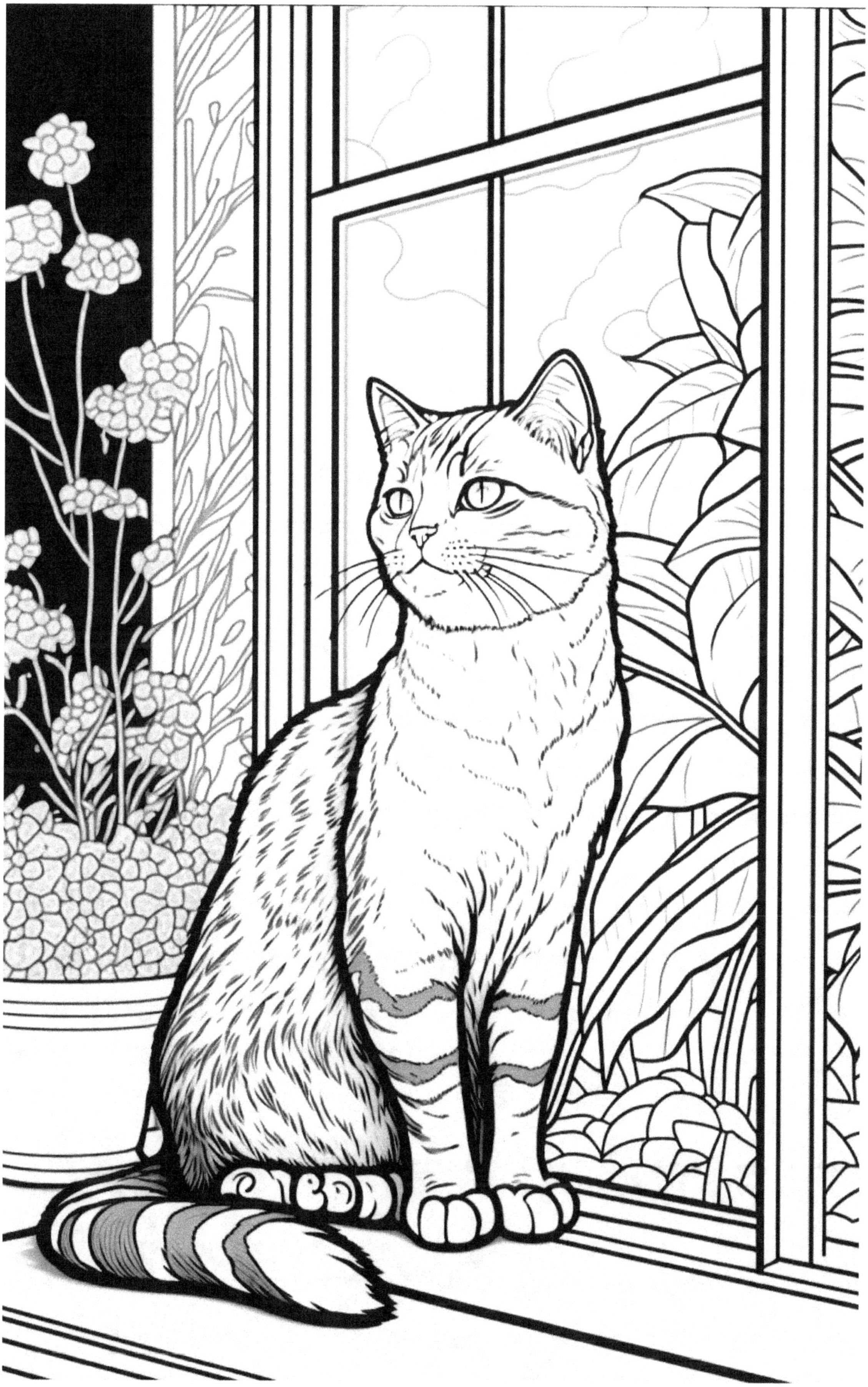

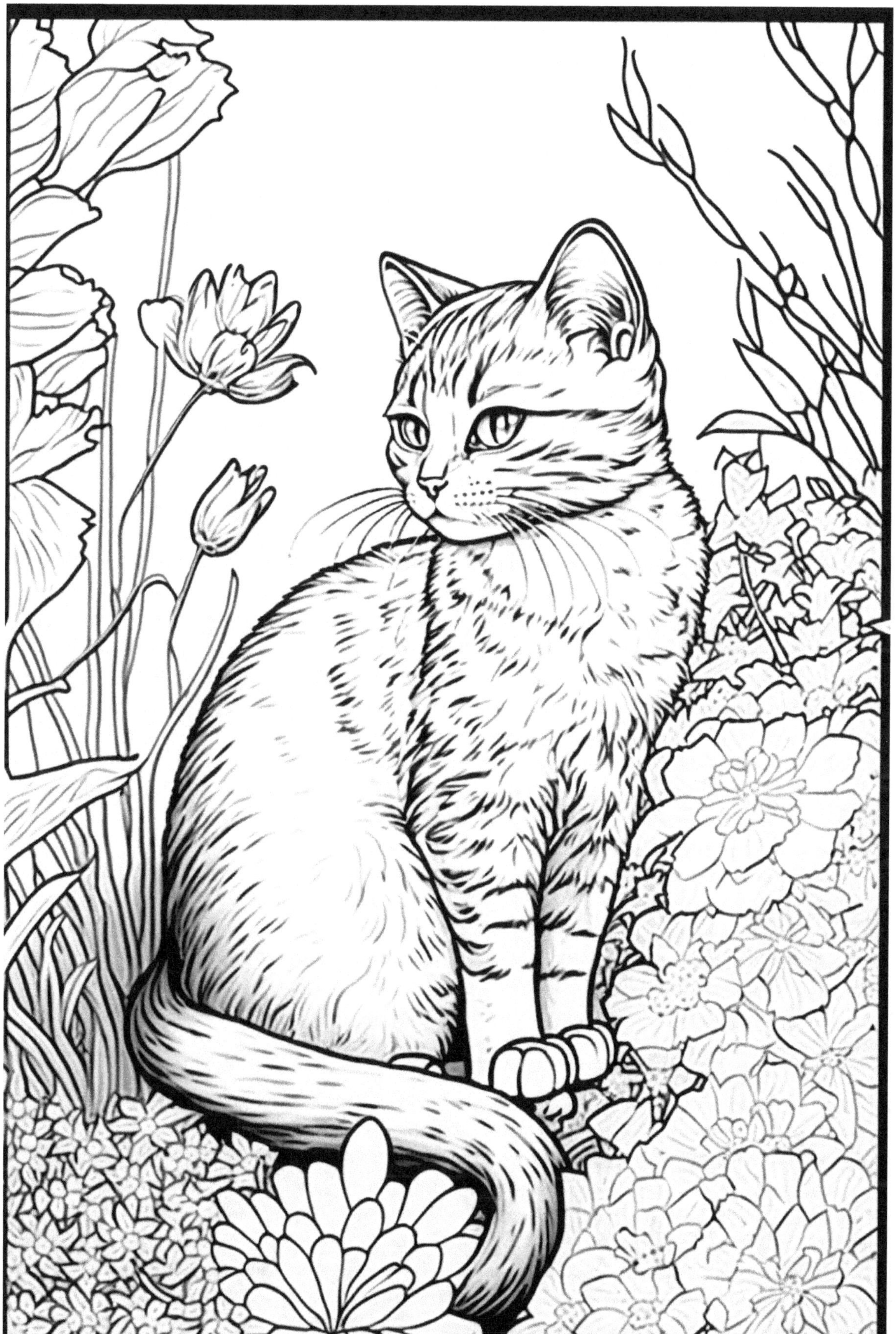

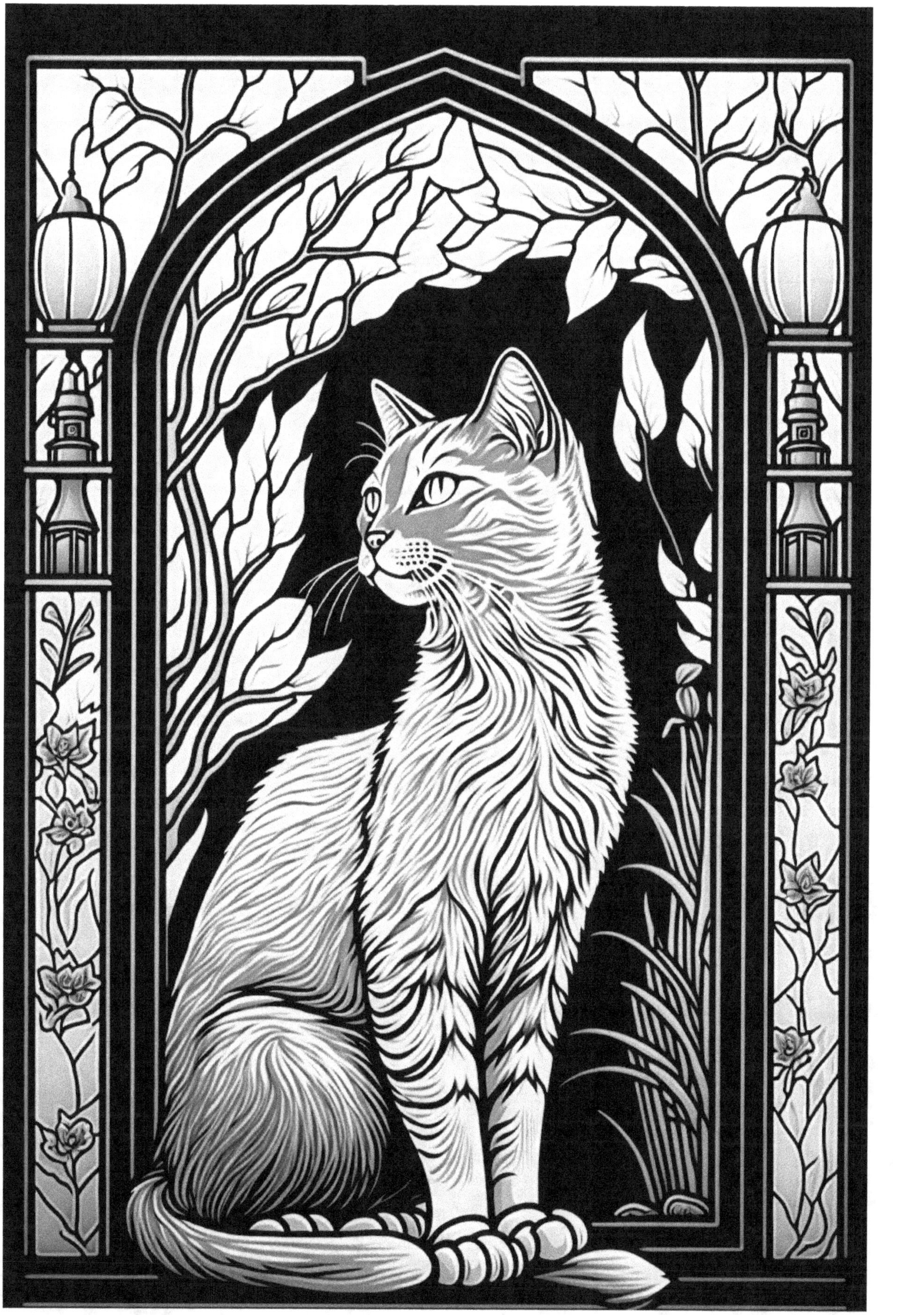

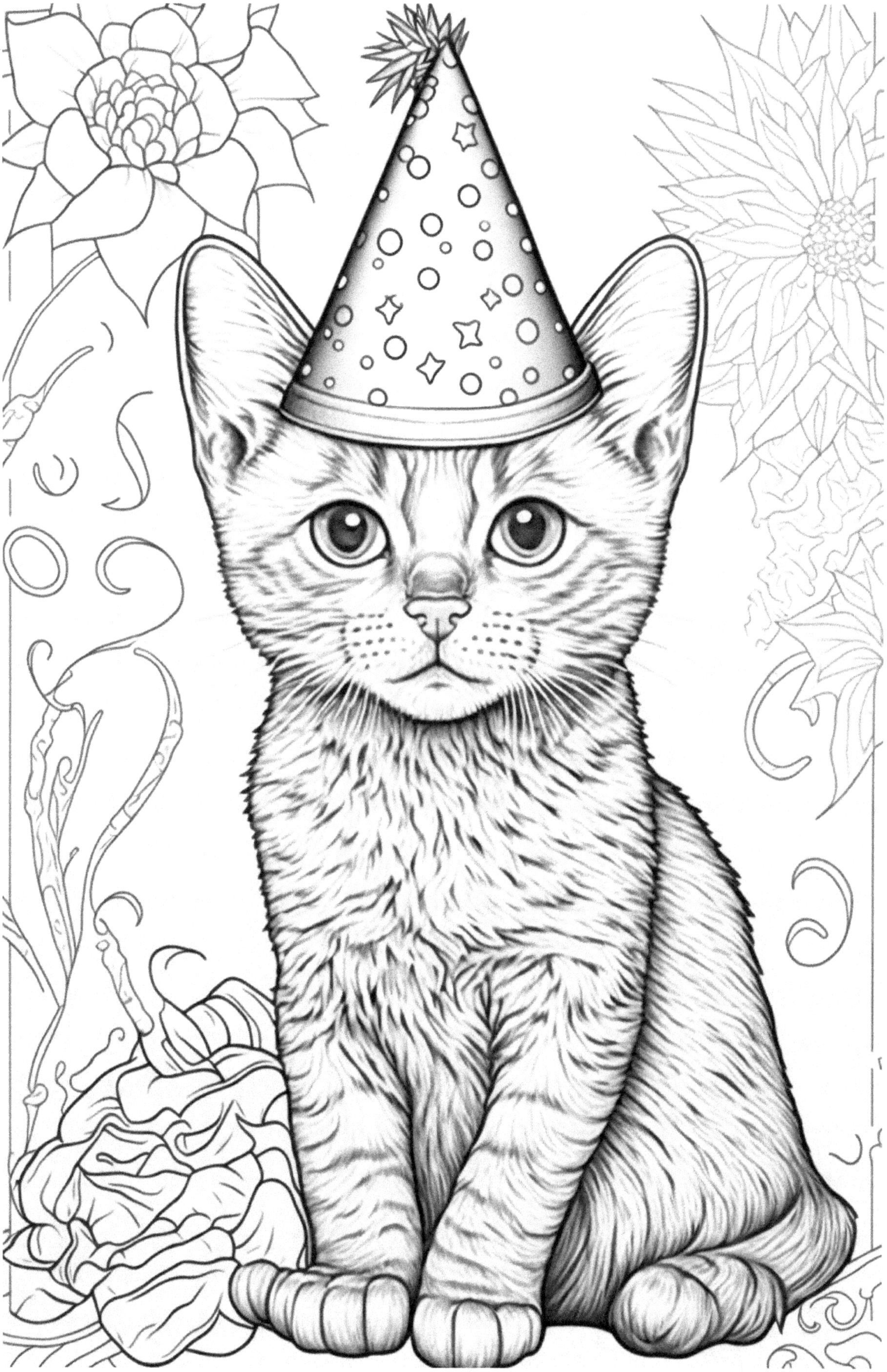

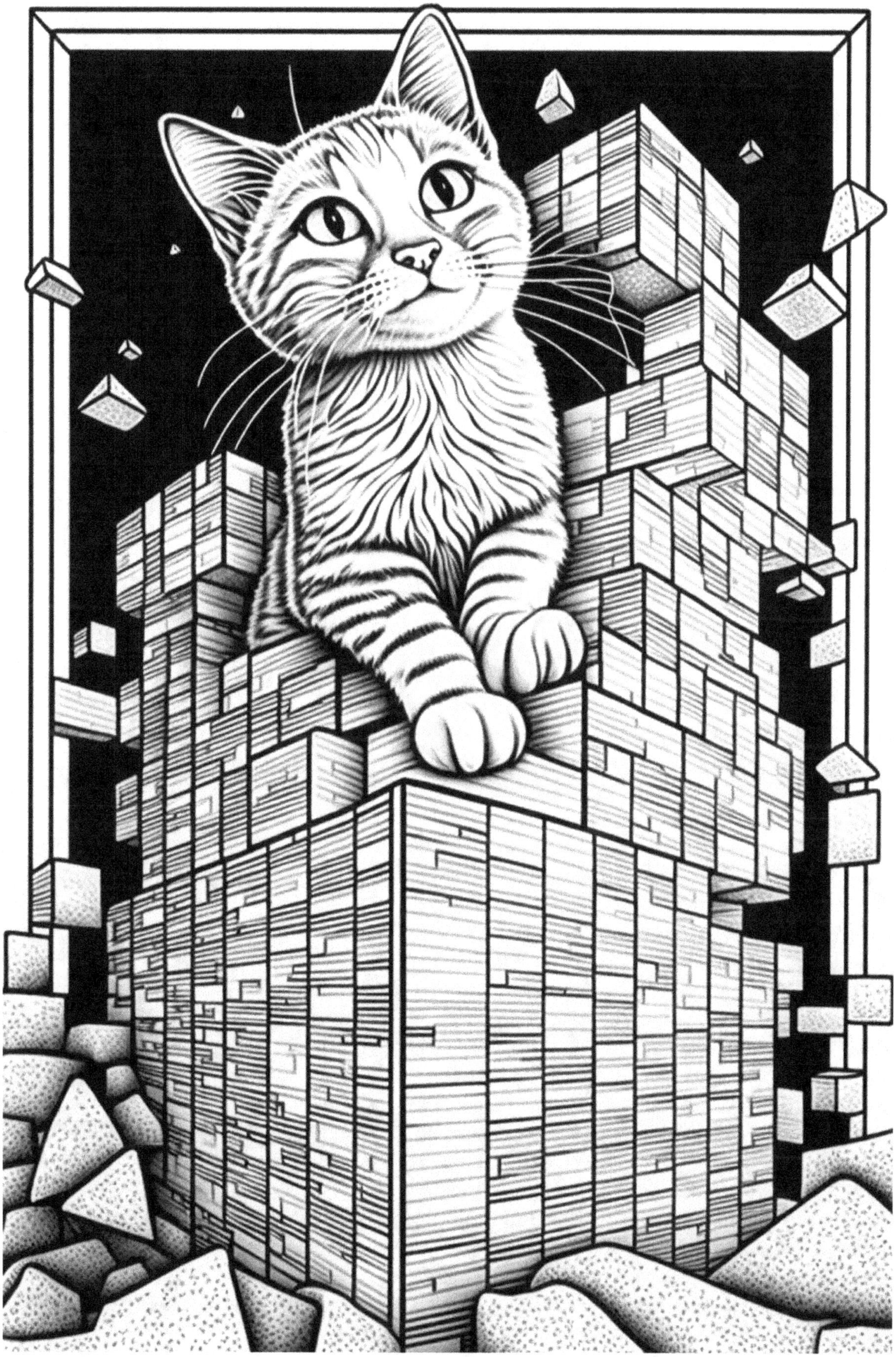

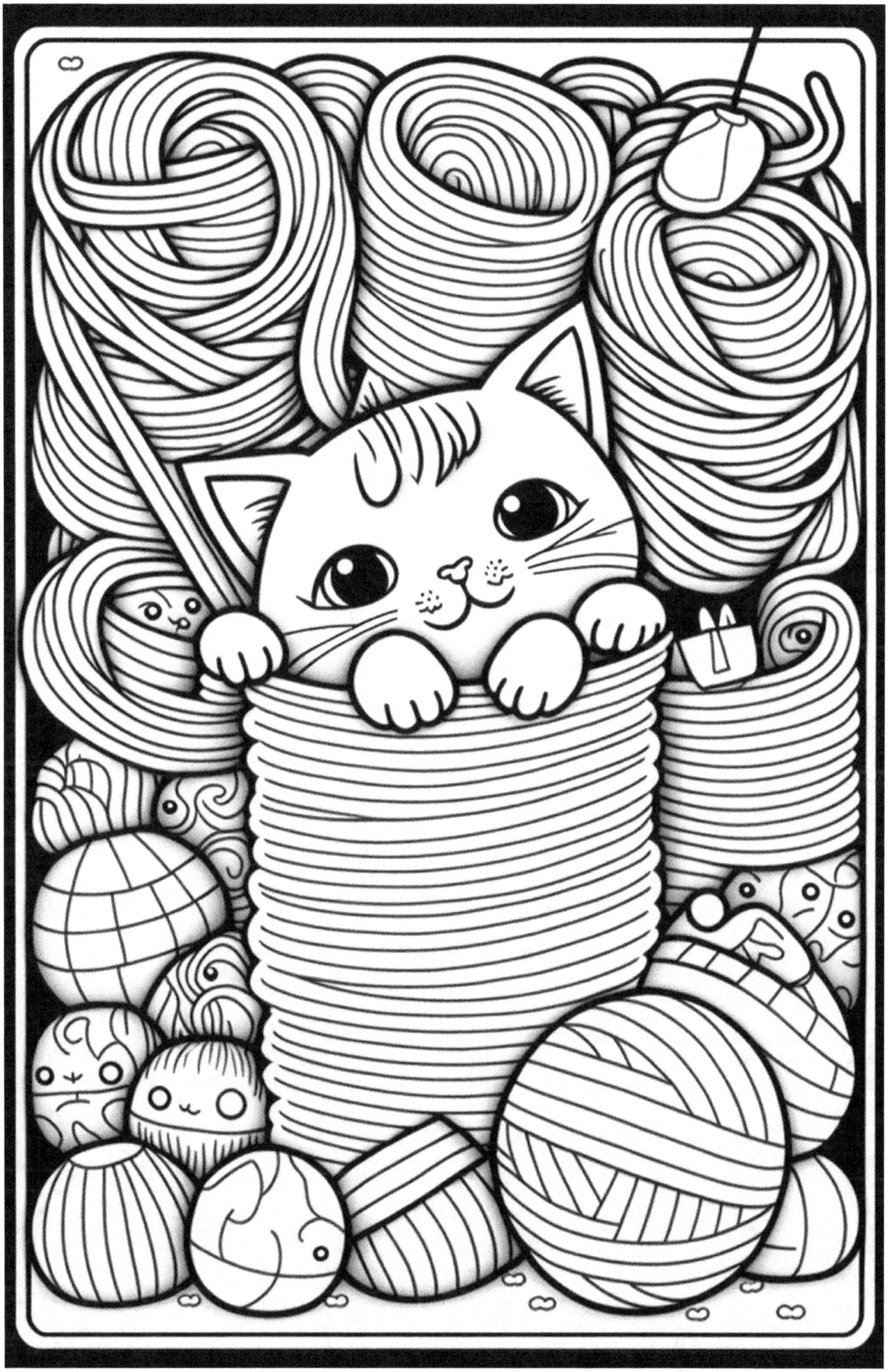

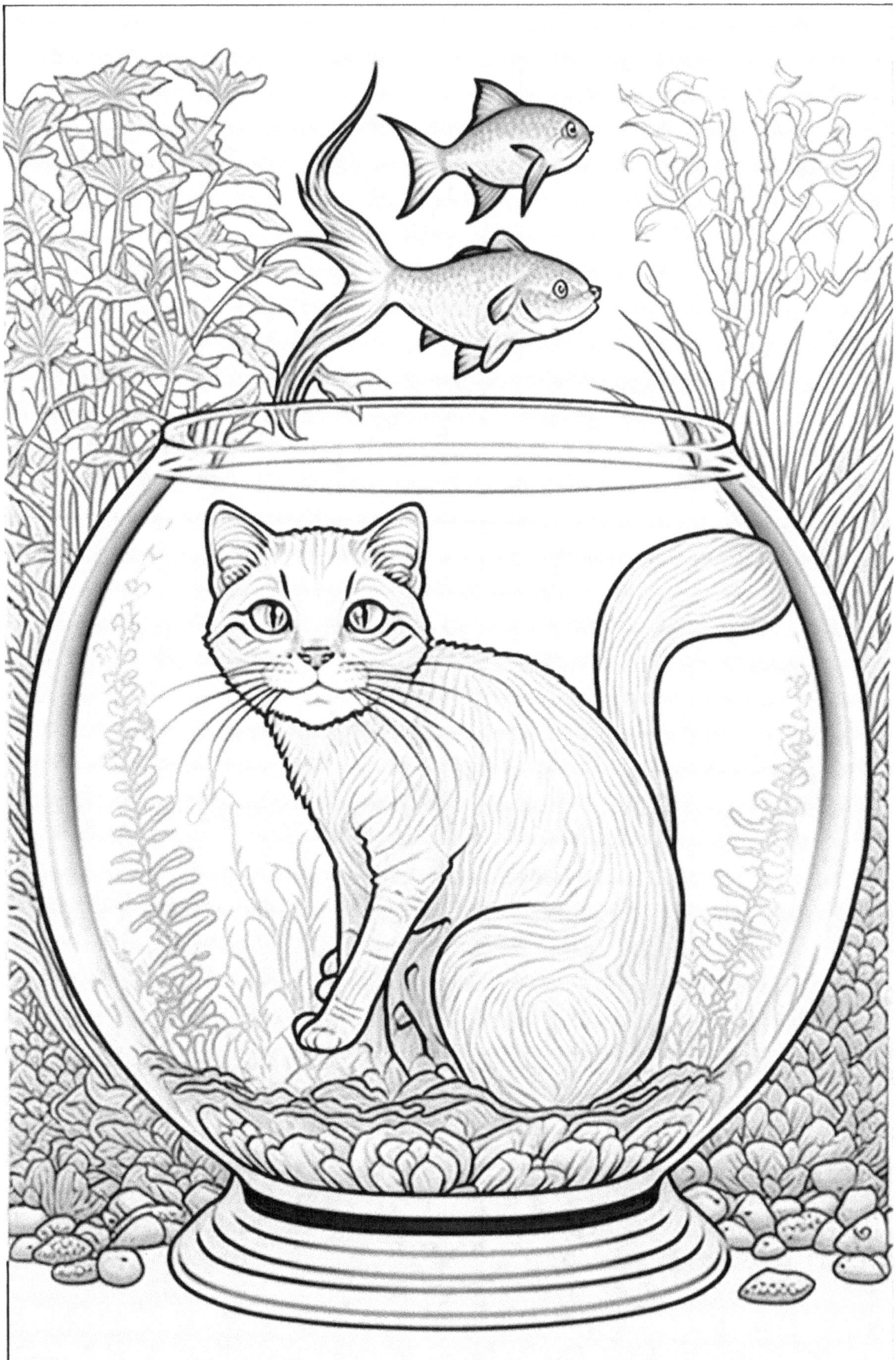

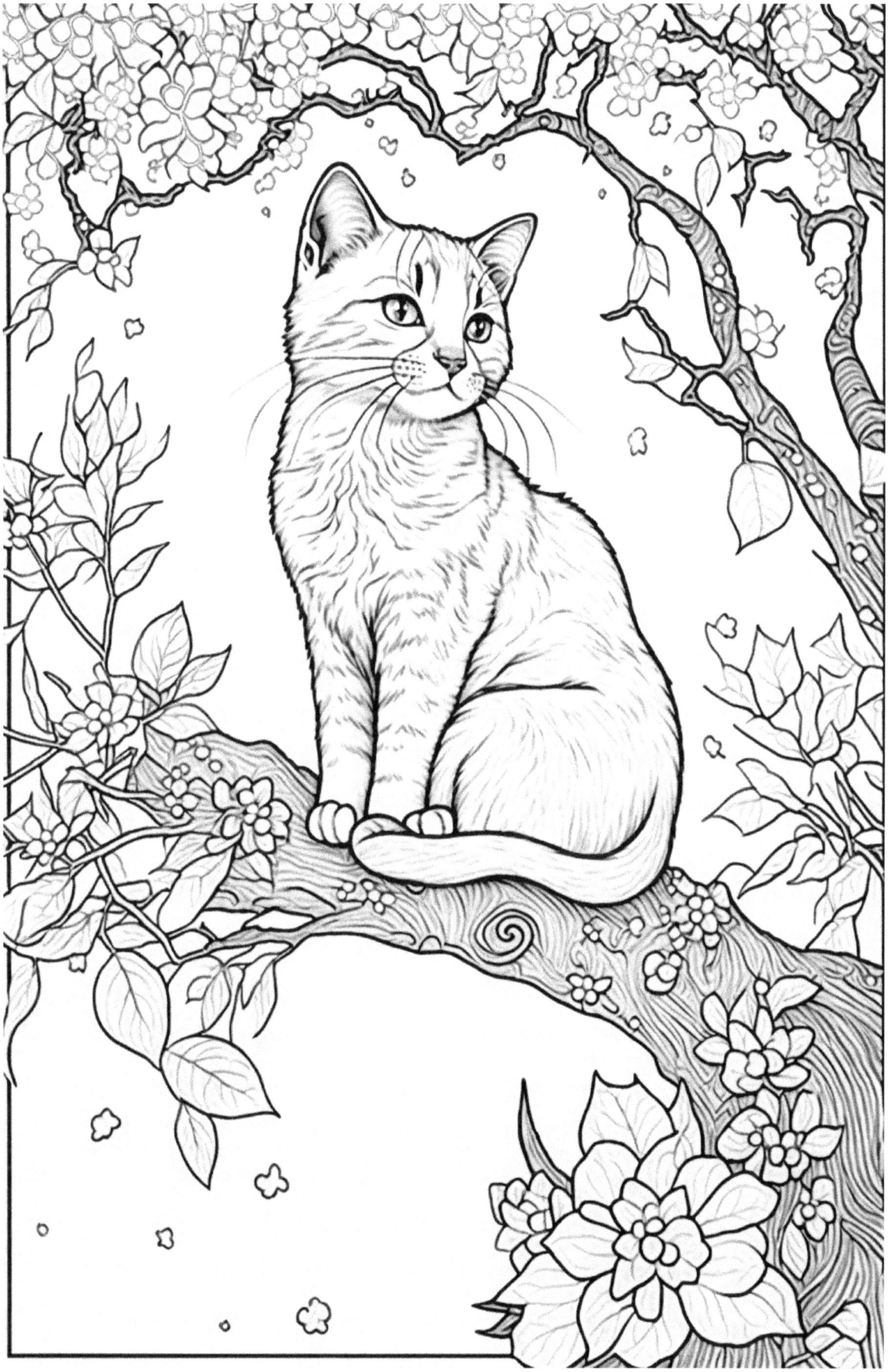

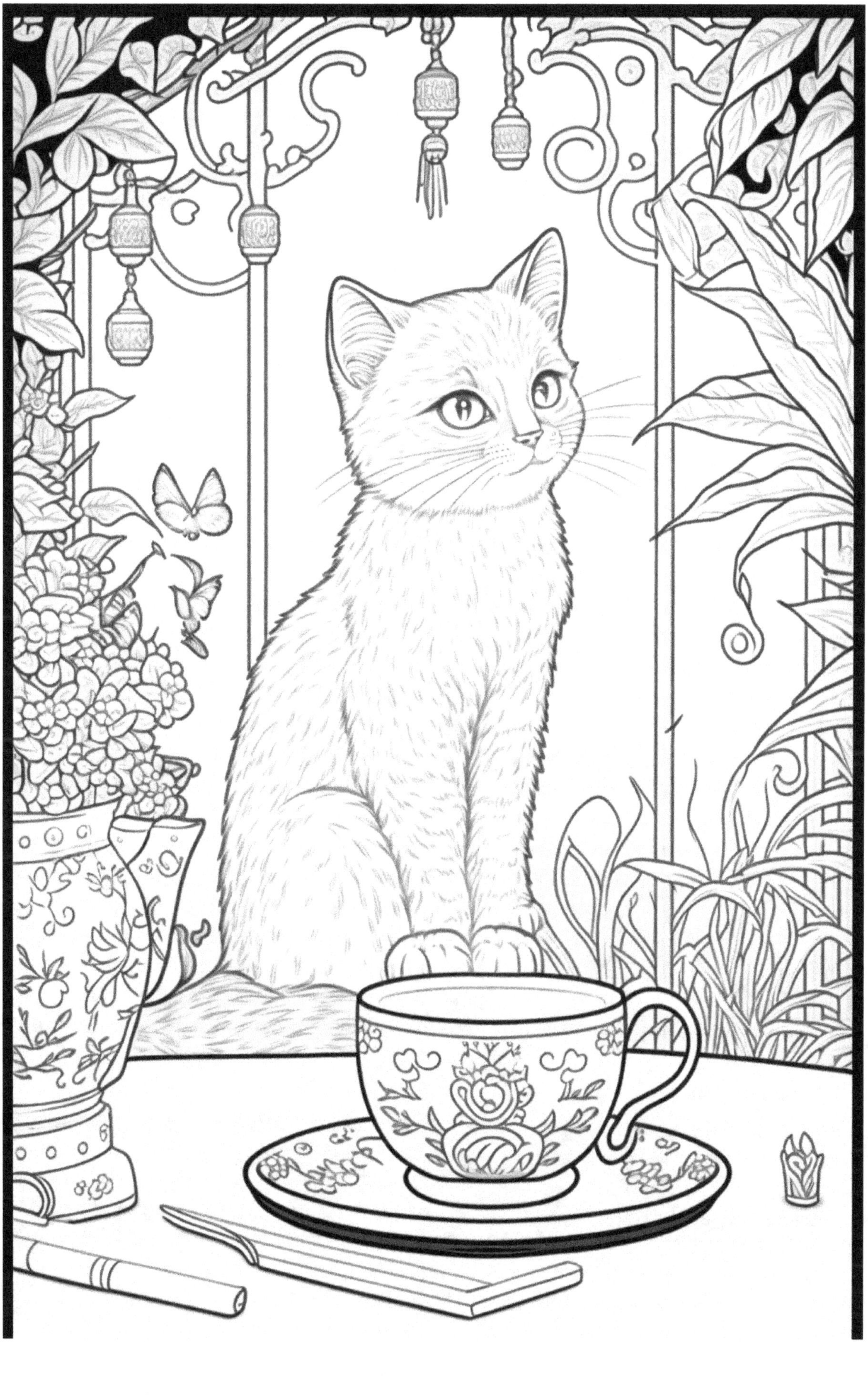

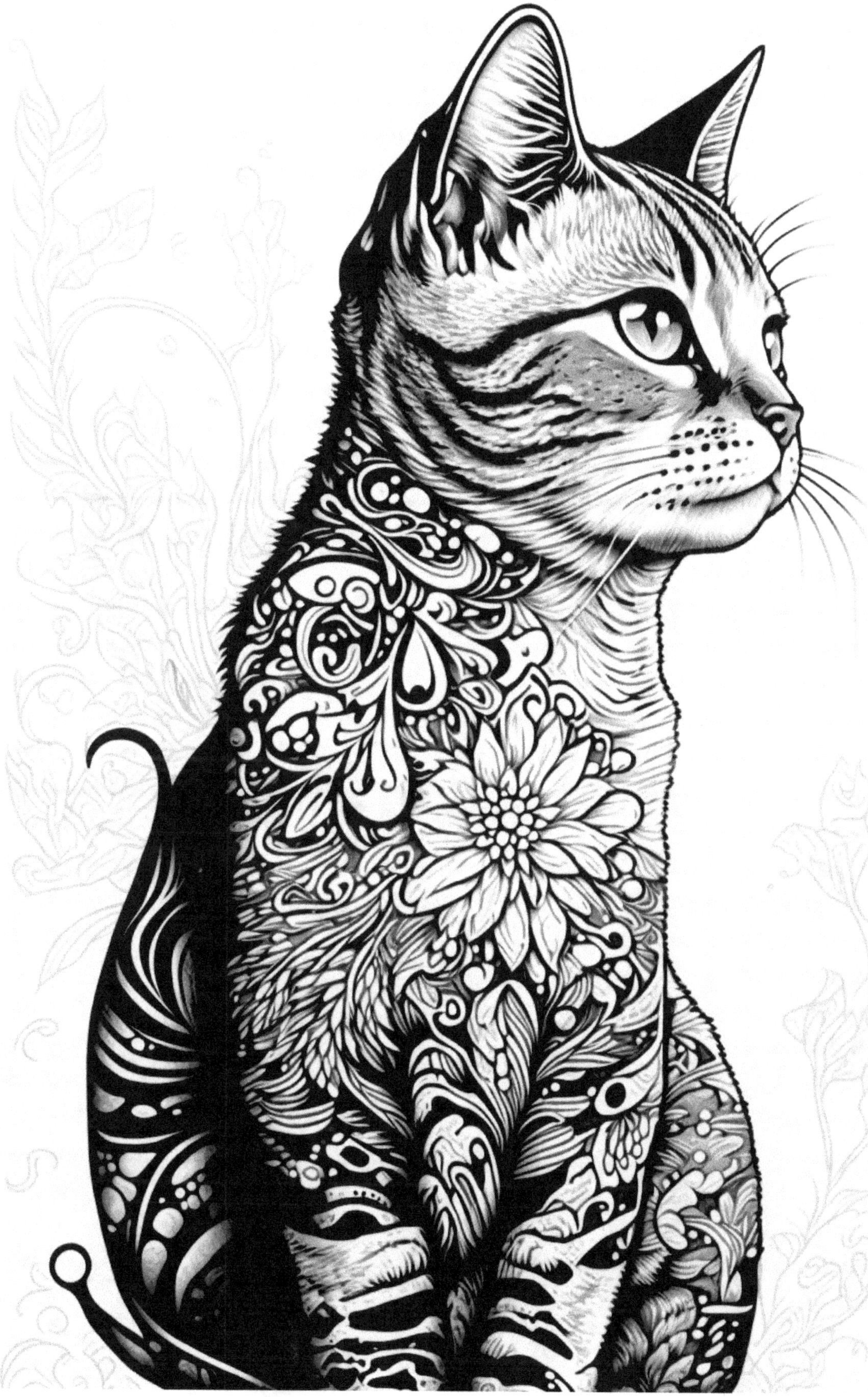

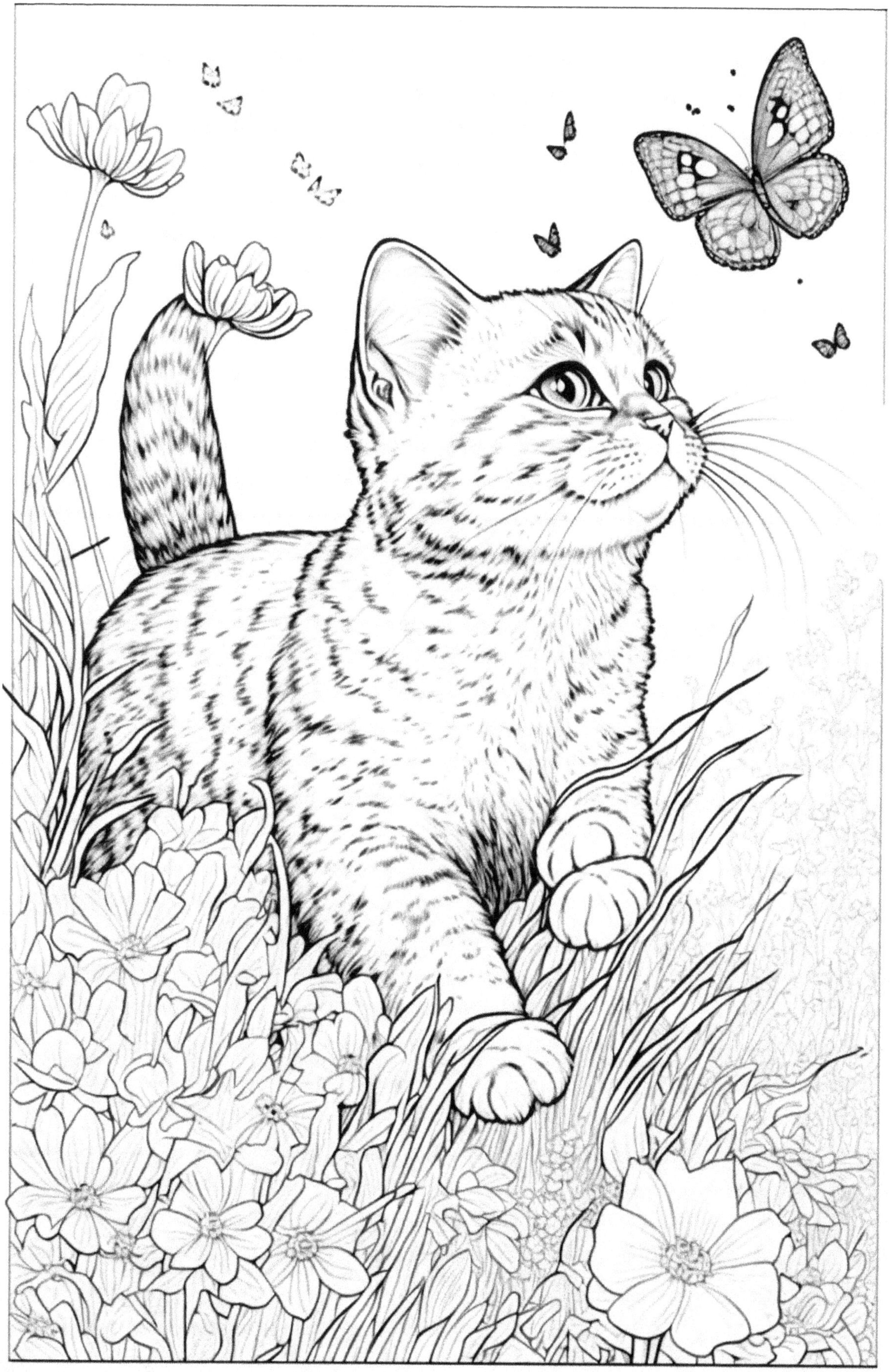

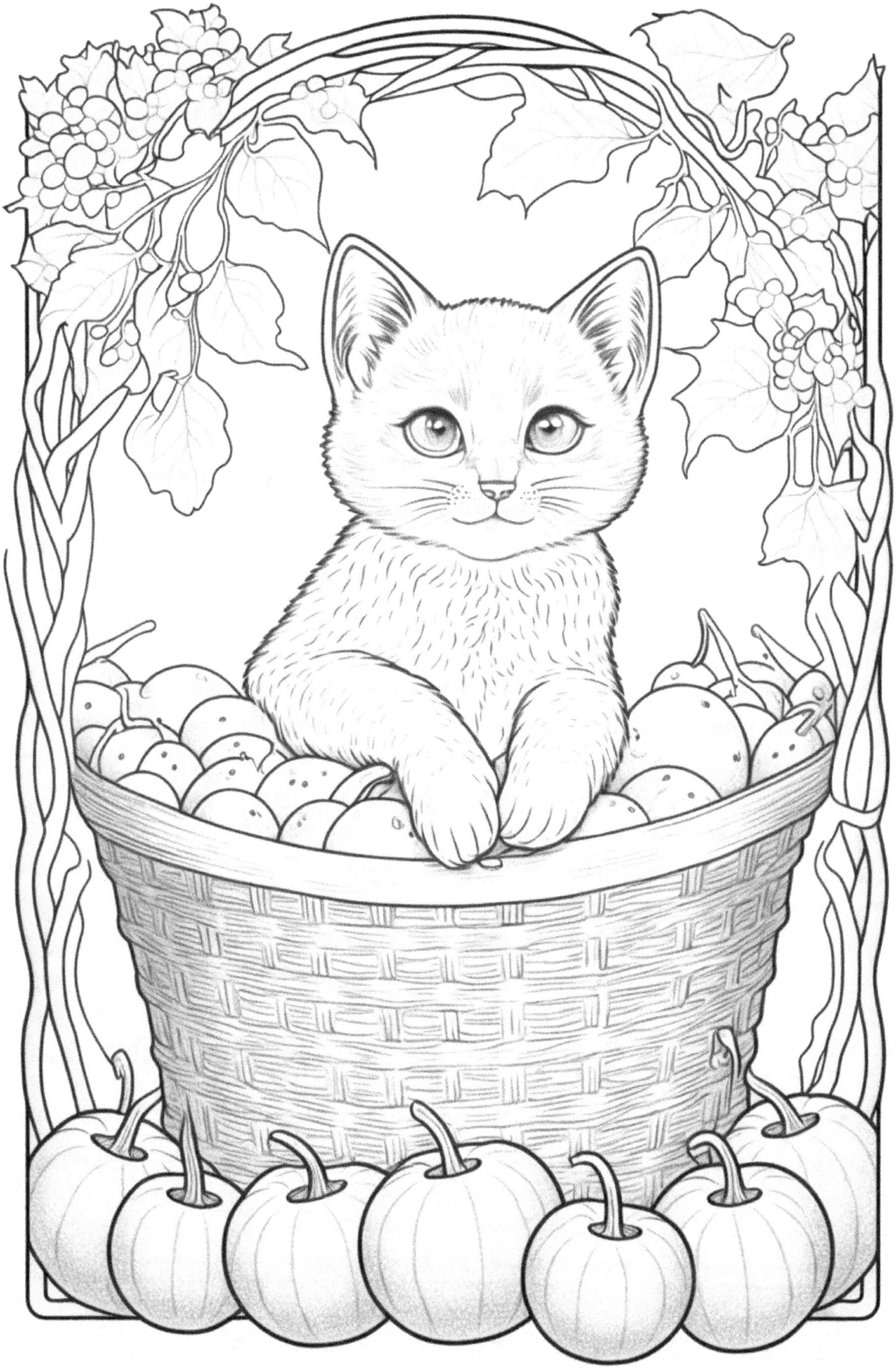

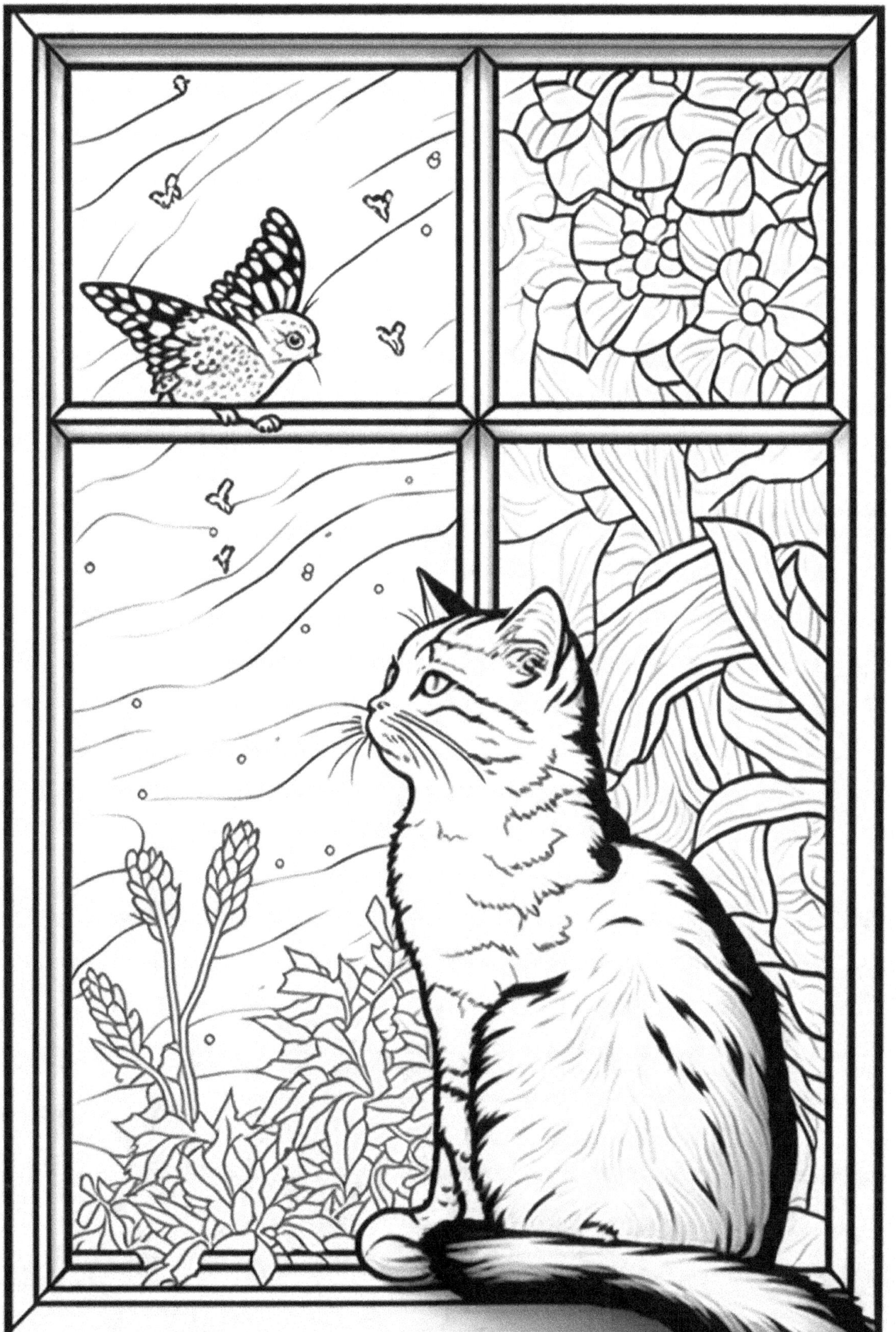

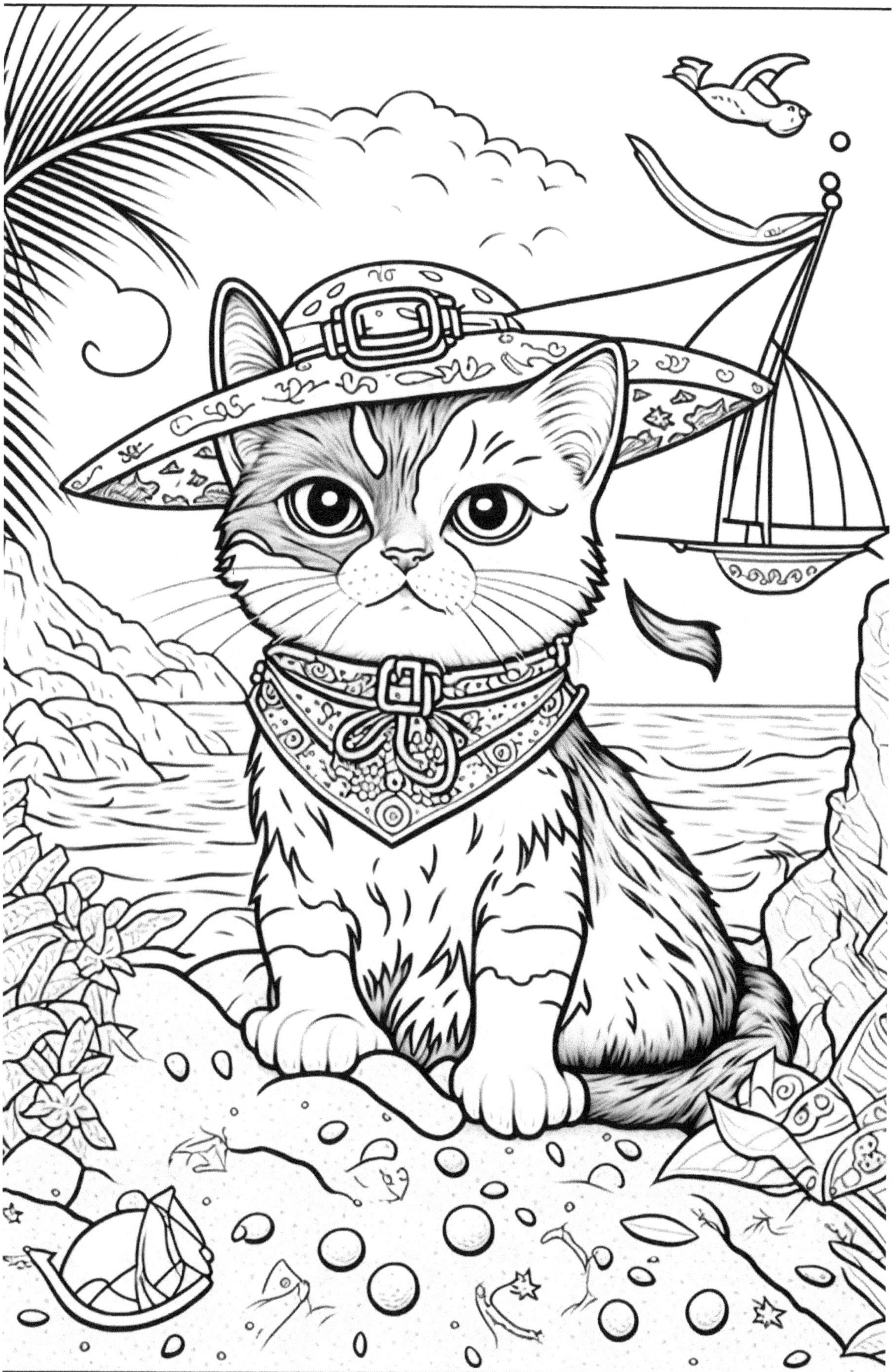

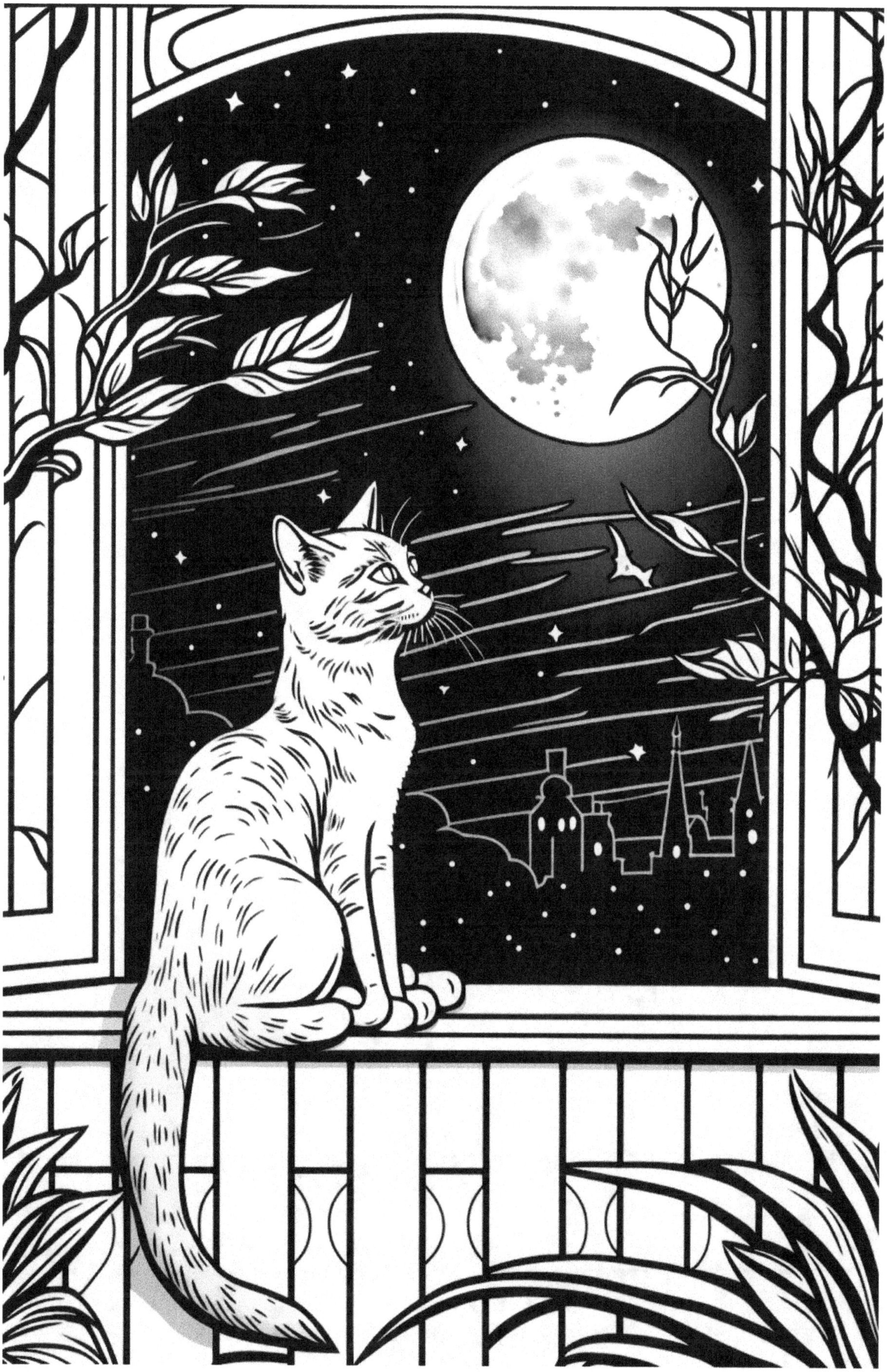

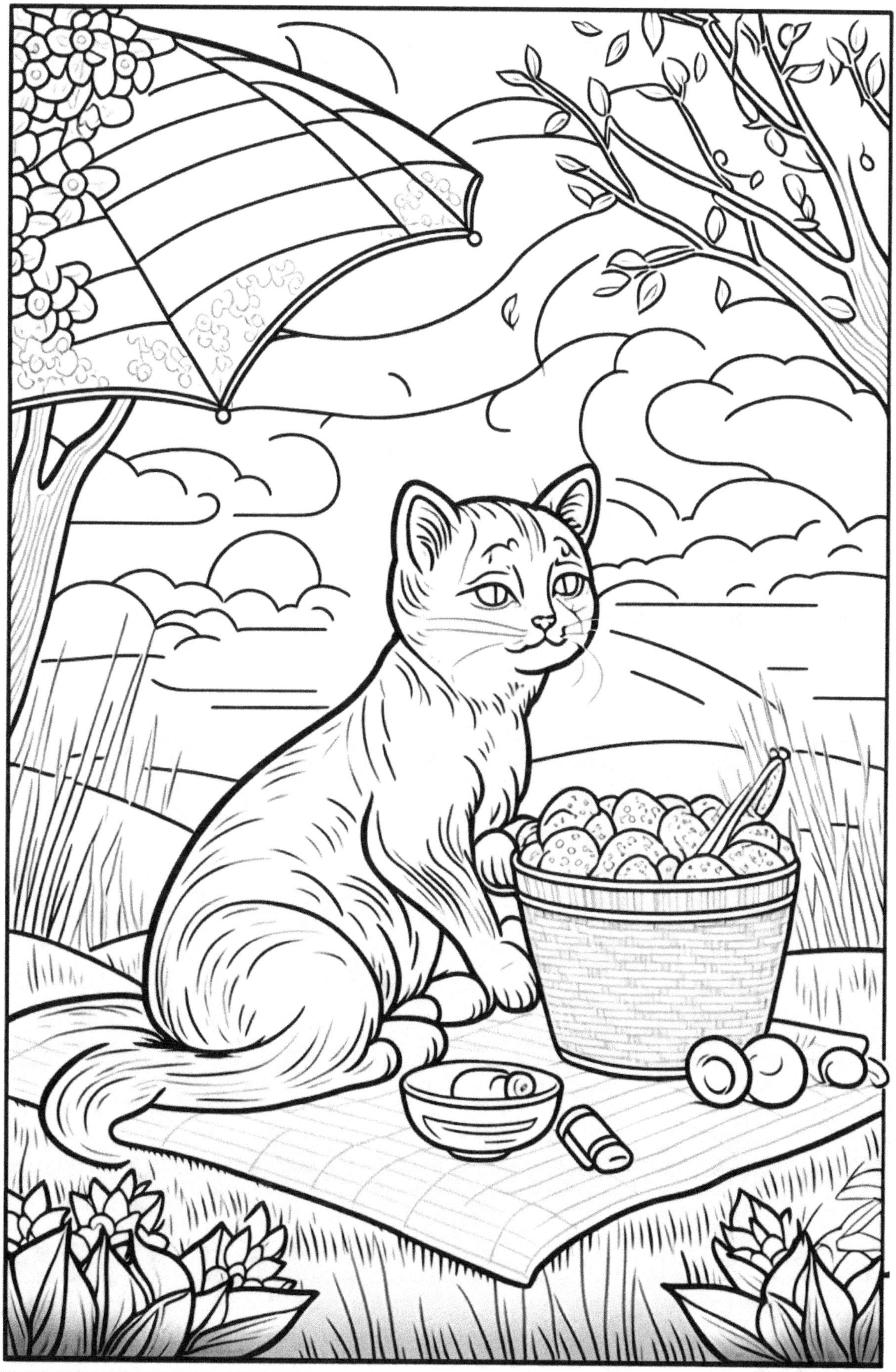

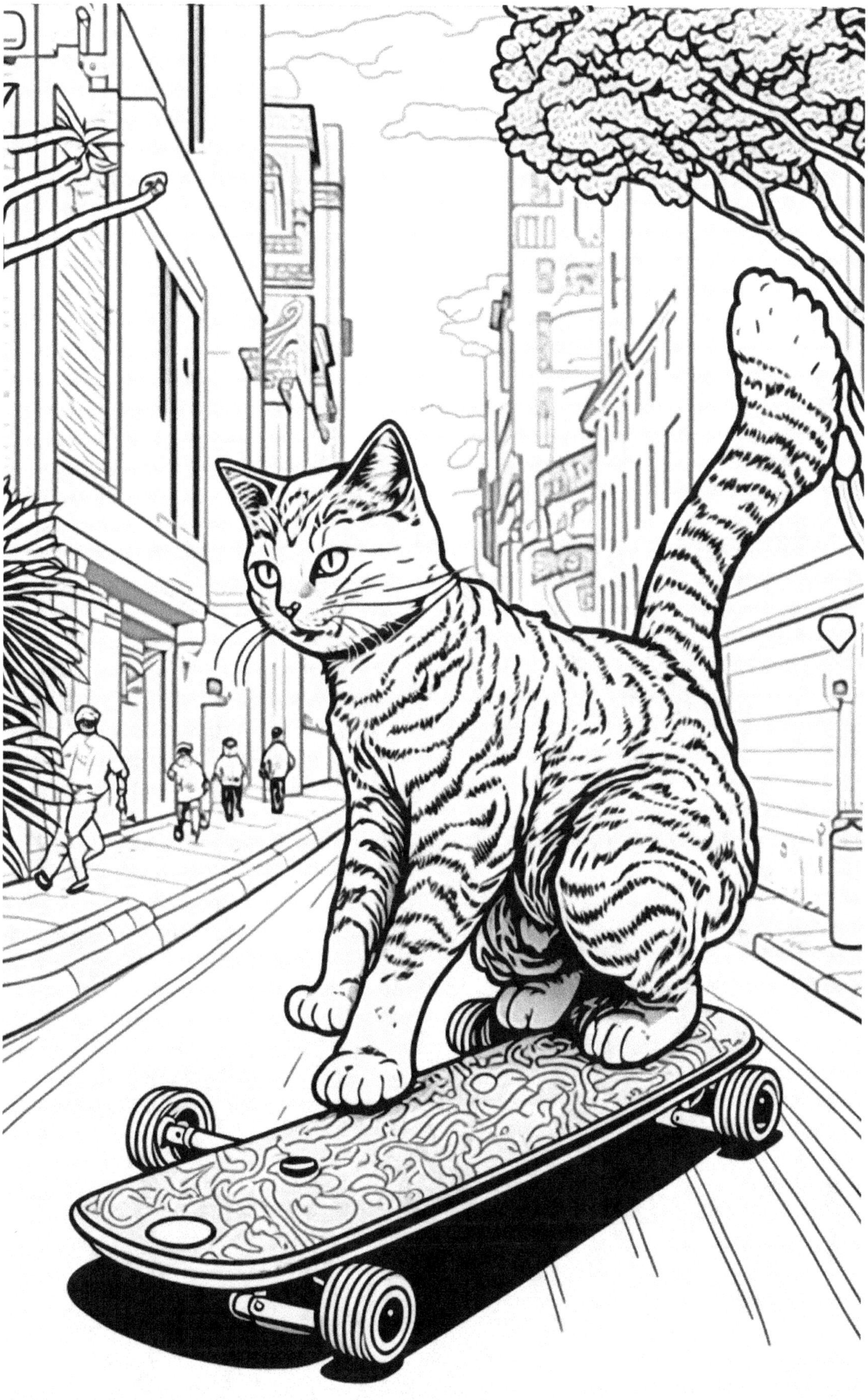

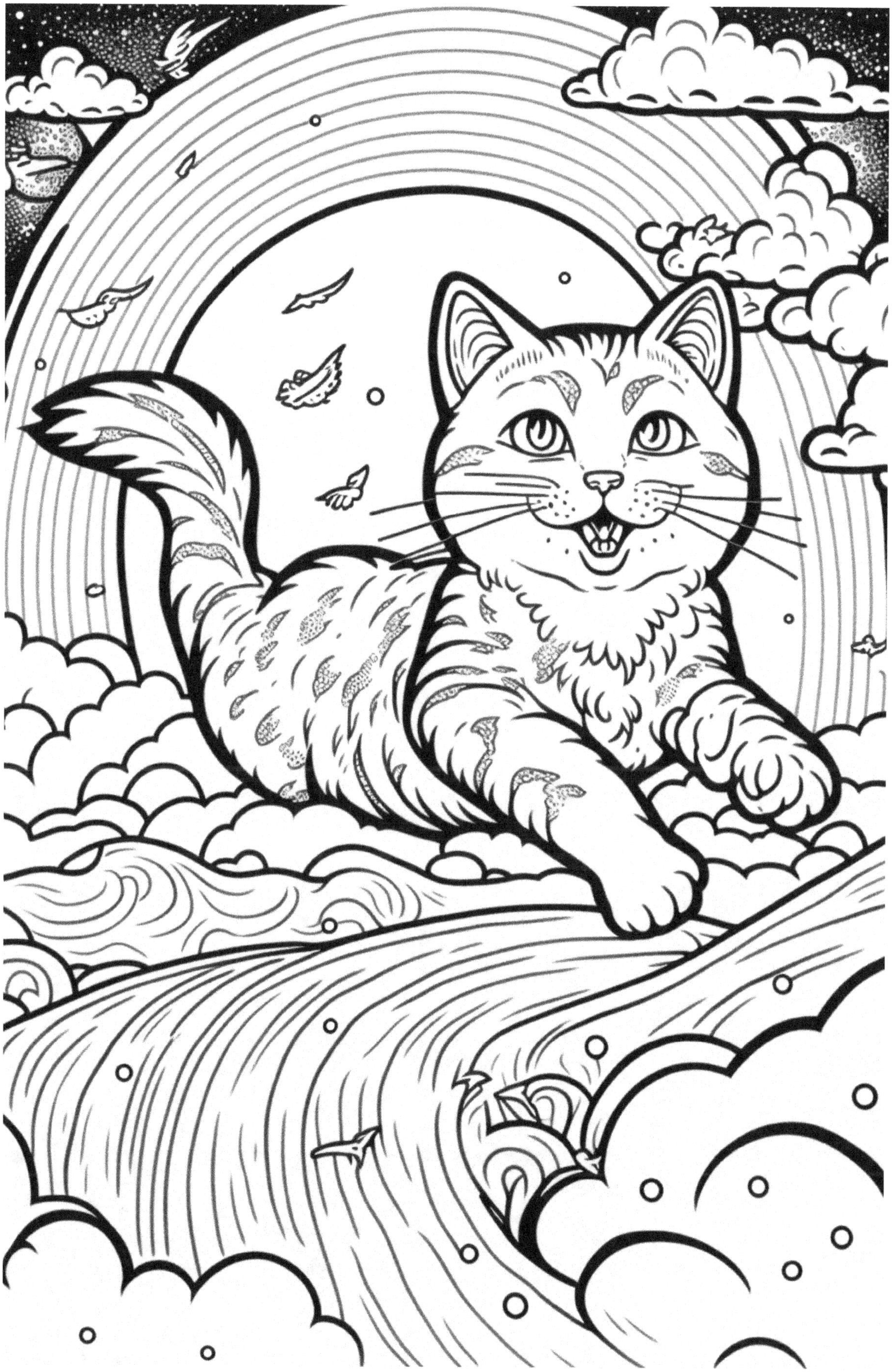

www.ingramcontent.com/pod-product-compliance
Lightning Source LLC
Chambersburg PA
CBHW081711220526
45467CB00034B/2773
9798378823970